Curiosity Didn't Kill The Cat

Tyreek Houston

First Edition

Editing by Joshua Yarbrough

DEDICATION

This book is dedicated to everyone who's played a crucial role in my life in helping me become the man I am today. It's also dedicated to all the life-long learners around the world. It's especially dedicated to anyone that's ever believed that they were destined for more, destined for greatness.
Let your inner light shine and nurture it with love.

CONTENTS

PREFACE

After years of following and using my curiosity as a tool to help achieve my goals, I've decided to share my journey and experiences to show others how they can do the same. Curiosity, combined with emotional intelligence, can make any journey a little bit easier, especially when you have an end goal in mind. One important life lesson I've learned is that nothing great happens overnight and all big things start small. In this book, you'll learn how to use the small gift of curiosity to develop a mindset of life-long learning. Every day is an opportunity to learn, so why not learn things that feed your own personal interests. The world is yours for the taking, all you must do is reach out and grab it.

This book is dedicated to my loving mother, Tamara, my sister, TaRae, my amazing grandparents, Lizzie and Eddie Cleveland, the Houston family, and to all my friends from elementary school and beyond.

INTRODUCTION

Curiosity killed the cat...

We've all heard this expression before, whether at an early age or a later age, it's ran its course into our ears. It's a common saying that most people can agree to hearing or actually saying, which makes it very acceptable by society. But have you ever asked yourself what does this old saying actually mean? Where it stems from? Or why it is so common? The implications of what this old saying means suggest many things that are counterproductive to learning and knowledge. The most obvious implication of what this old saying suggests is don't be curious. Now ask yourself, why would society not want you to be curious? In short and simple terms, if you know too much, you become a threat to the current system that is based on the principles of capitalism and oppression.

A system of human domestication; the same system we use on animals based on punishment and rewards. For example, if your dog has an accident in the house, it will be called "bad dog," at the very least, as a form of punishment. If your dog obeys, it will be rewarded with some kind of treat for good behavior. If this sounds familiar, it's because it was programmed in you since before you were able to say your first words.

The old saying *curiosity killed the cat* and the system we live in share some common things. For example, they're both unconsciously rooted into our memory. They can unconsciously shape our behavior and way of thinking because of the associations we draw from the punishment and reward system we know. They can also create fear, uncertainty and doubt, normally resulting in complacency in our actions, hindrance from personal growth, and discouragement from high aspirations. You must be able to shift your mindset to know that curiosity is an asset that allows you to put action behind questioning. An asset that guides your hearts desires. An asset that allows you to free your mind from the puppeteer that controls society without fear of consequences.

What's interesting about consequences is that they can be both positive and negative. We tend to only focus on negative consequences, but what about if we shift our attention to the positive ones? What if we knew curiosity didn't kill the cat? The beauty of curiosity is that everyone has it. When you're in pursuit of a goal and approach others humbly seeking information, curiosity is normally met with compassion. People are more likely to help you when curiosity is perceived. When used properly, curiosity can be a life-long companion to achieve any goal. Asking questions or seeking knowledge are both acts of curiosity that can lead you to meet your goals.

This book journey's through significant time periods in my life when curiosity was the key in helping me take action and leading me to my goals. It also teaches how emotional intelligence and curiosity complement each other, while providing guidance on when and where curiosity ought to be used. Experience is one of our best teachers, and I hope that by sharing my experiences it can enable others to take action to achieve their personal and professional goals by staying curious.

1

CURIOSITY

Where would we be in the world if we didn't remain curious? Would technological advancements like WiFi or Blockchain even exist? Would traveling by air be an option? Would the thought of airplanes even enter our minds? Probably not. Most of the breakthrough discoveries and remarkable inventions throughout history, from flints for starting a fire to self-driving cars, have something in common: They are the result of curiosity (Harvard Business Review).

According to Webster's dictionary, curiosity is defined as "the desire to know, inquisitive interest in others' concerns, or interest leading to inquiry." To have a desire to know, is to have the will to learn. Learning is a natural process of life; think about how much you've learned since birth. Speaking, walking, running, eating, reading, writing…everything you're capable of doing at this very moment in time was a learned experience.

At the age of 5, I can remember asking my parents so many questions that I'm sure they got annoyed with me. "How did you learn to drive Mom?" or "Why do I have to stay on the sidewalk riding my bike Grandma?" And the infamous childhood question, "do I really have to go to school?" Driven by curiosity, people seek to explore the world in different ways. At no time in life is curiosity more powerful than in early childhood (Dr. Bruce D. Perry). School field trips are a way to help nurture and encourage curiosity. Have you ever taken a school field trip to the aquarium and wanted to know everything about every animal? Or maybe a trip to a science museum and wanted to try every attraction there? If you can connect to either of these examples, they all have something in common; they're the result of being curious or interested, leading to inquiry as Webster defines it.

As a child in the early 1990s, there was always one thing that constantly triggered my curiosity, which was technology. I grew up in a tiny one-bedroom apartment in southern New Jersey with my mother and father. While my parents worked, I spent most of my time being babysat by my grandmother. One day, my Mom decided to work from home, and I asked her, curiously "am I still going to Grandma's house?" She replied, "no son, I'm working from home today." This was the first time I ever heard of that concept. My mind didn't know what else to do other than ask questions. "What's that? Can you do it all the time? How come

2

you don't work from home more often?" Mom answered every question as lovingly as she could. I felt content and understood everything she told me. I thought all my questions were done until I saw her take out her work laptop and get on the Internet. You can imagine how amazed I was. Picture a young child finding out what working from home is, on top of witnessing the Internet for the first time in less than 10 minutes. I probably distracted my Mom from work for another 30 minutes, but she had taken the time to answer all my questions. By the end of our conversation, technology had inspired me in more ways than I could've imagined. Today, I work in the technology industry as a User Experience Researcher. How did I get there? I followed my curiosity.

From a young child, to a young adult, I never let my curiosity fade. The world is filled with obstacles that will try to challenge your curiosity with normality. One way to overcome any obstacle, is by staying curious and questioning everything. People will give you advice based on their own experience, but what if you ask someone a question that's beyond their own experience? What useful advice can they give other than advice from a relatable experience? What if they don't have a relatable experience for your questions? Will they point you in the direction of someone that can answer it, or will they tell you they don't know? It's important to question things and let curiosity guide you, so that you're not solely led by other people's words or opinions. One person's truth may not be another person's truth. Just like one person's experience may not reflect another's. When you don't accept other people's words or opinions as truth, you allow yourself to critically process information and form your own opinion. In short, you give yourself a choice to accept or deny someone else's truth as your own. Letting curiosity guide you is your roadmap to intellectual freedom, critical thinking and personal development.

Intellectual freedom is your ticket to all sorts of information. According to the American Library Association, intellectual freedom is "the right of every individual to both seek and receive information from all points of view without restriction." It provides free access to all expressions of ideas through which any and all sides of a question, cause, or movement may be explored. Intellectual freedom is the basis for our democratic system. We expect our people to be self-governors, but to do so responsibly, our people must be well informed. Censorship is the suppression of ideas and information that certain persons—individuals, groups and or government officials—find objectionable or dangerous. It's no more complicated than someone saying, "don't let anyone read this book, or buy that magazine, or view that film, because I object to it!" Censors try to use the power of the state to impose their view of what is truthful and appropriate, or offensive and objectionable, on everyone else. Censors pressure public institutions, like libraries, to suppress and remove from public access information they judge inappropriate or dangerous, so that no one else has the chance to read or view the material and make up their own minds about it. Have you ever wanted to read a book, or watch a special documentary, but then one day, you couldn't find it anymore? You can thank censorship. It happens all around us, all the time, with or without our knowledge. To live in a democracy is to allow people to be self-governed, but they must also be allowed to be well informed. Misinformed people represent a tainted democracy. A democracy that doesn't allow its people to access, receive, hold and spread information of all kinds is inherently flawed. Being curious allows you to search and ask valuable questions to receive valuable answers and information. Knowing that censorship happens all around us makes me wonder why. What about you?

2

EMOTIONAL INTELLIGENCE

S taying curious is one side of the coin for personal development and emotional intelligence is the other. According to information from *Psychology Today*, emotional intelligence refers to the ability to identify and manage one's own emotions, as well as the emotions of others. It's generally said to include at least three skills; the ability to identify and name one's own emotions, the ability to harness those emotions and apply them to tasks like thinking and problem solving, and the ability to manage emotions, which includes both regulating one's own emotions when necessary and helping others to do the same. We should all be able to manage our emotions, as well as empathize with others. That's what being human is. We are emotional beings. You may be asking yourself, what does emotional intelligence have to do with curiosity? It's a good thing that you're questioning this, because it's the backbone of curiosity. They complement one another. To be curious without emotional intelligence is to seek or ask questions that may seem offensive to others without concern. For example, imagine a White person at an all Black cookout. The sun is shining and the music's just right. It's time to eat and the food's amazing. Everybody's enjoying their food and then all of a sudden, the White person watches a few Black people putting hot sauce on their food. They ask their nearby Black friend "does everyone put hot sauce on their food?" You can imagine what kind of response that question would get. Although it may have seemed like an innocent question, it could be very offensive to the ones being asked, and you may receive a response you didn't expect. Context, awareness, and emotional intelligence matters when being curious.

In the 6th grade, I received my first "F" on a test in school. I had just entered middle school and the learning curve was steeper than I expected. If my Mom hadn't seen me studying the week of the test, I would've been able to hide the fact that I just got my first F, but that wasn't the case. I dreaded coming home that day for the simple fact that I knew once my Mom got home, she was going to ask me how I did. Questions frantically raced through my head. How is she going to react? Am I going to get grounded? Will she be upset at me? I didn't know what to expect other than a parent who wouldn't expect her son to bring home an "F". I believed this was a situation I couldn't control —

so I thought. By envisioning how she would react, I thought of ways I could tell her I didn't pass that would evoke a concerned response, rather than a surprised one. "I got an F", no... "I didn't do so good", nah... "I didn't pass", won't work... "I don't know what happened", BINGO. Telling my Mom I don't know what happened would for sure trigger concerned responses. If I was the parent, my response to hearing that would be "what do you mean?" Thinking from this perspective, I asked myself how I would respond to my mother if she asked me what do I mean. Should I explain how I prepared for the test and didn't get the results I expected? Or should I just say I didn't do so good? I chose to explain how I prepared for the test and didn't get the score that I expected because it showed the level of effort that I put into preparing for the test. It also showed a general concern for my grade, not being satisfied with an F. I hoped that this approach would also make my Mom as concerned as I was. All I could do now was test the theory.

My Mom got home around 7:00 pm, a few hours after I did. "Hey Mom," I said in a calm manner. "Hey son, how are you" she said with her usual ecstatic tone. "I'm ok," I replied. "How did you do on your test? I saw you studying this week" she asked with no hesitation. I replied, "I don't know what happened." She replied, "what do you mean?" I explained how much I studied, how much I practiced, how prepared I felt before taking the test, how confident I felt about the answers I marked, and how shocked I was receiving an F as my score. As I finished talking, my Mom put her hand on my shoulder and gently said "I know this isn't like you. Don't worry about this. It's just one test. There's plenty more you'll have, and I know you'll do better on all of them. Middle school is little different than elementary school. If you need extra help don't be shy to ask your teachers or even me. That's what we're here for."

If there was ever a time in my life when I felt comforted and relieved at the same time, it was then. By putting myself in my mother's shoes and understanding how she would feel after hearing I didn't do well on a test, I was able to think of the best way to tell her the news. Not only did she show concern, she gave me great advice, motivated me and offered to help when I need it. With a little emotional intelligence, I was able to transform a situation of uncertainty into a situation of comfort and concern. The uncertainty overwhelmed me when I first saw the grade, but I was able to manage my emotions as well as the emotional response it could evoke from my Mom. By being aware of how my words could trigger different types of responses, I was able to think critically about my word choice and make a conscious decision on how to articulate myself. I may have failed my first test in Middle school, but I definitely passed the emotional intelligence one.

3

FORWARD-THINKING

As my educational journey continued, I started to seriously think about what my future would look like. In my hometown, Willingboro, NJ, students had four high schools to choose to attend. Willingboro High, Rancocas Valley, or Burlington County Institute of Technology (BCIT) at Westampton or Medford. With so many choices, I wanted to position myself to be in a place that would allow me to get ahead of the curve. Somewhere that I could start my career early while still having the option to go to college. Have you ever thought about what your life would be like in the next 5 years? Or planned the next 10 years in advance? If so, then you're a forward-thinker. According to information from Webster's dictionary, "forward-thinking" is *"thinking about and planning for the future; forward-looking."* When you think about and plan for the future, you allow yourself to plan strategically while being open to possibilities. You're able to connect the dots to see the larger picture and it all starts by letting curiosity lead you.

After much consideration, I chose to attend Burlington County Institute of Technology (BCIT) at Westampton. The institute is a well-known four-year countywide vocational technical public high school that offers students a variety of programs and majors. It also offers practical trade experience, internship opportunities, a certificate of major completion upon graduating, and recognition by universities around the world. This school aligned to my future goals perfectly. After passing the entrance exam, it was off to the races to explore what major I wanted to pursue.

First year students get the option to explore their top four majors within the first month of attendance. I chose to explore Culinary Arts, Auto Mechanics, Graphic Design and Pre-Engineering. I liked Culinary Arts, but I didn't see where I would go in the future with it. I knew Auto Mechanics wasn't for me because I like to use my mind more than my hands. Graphic Design was interesting, but I lacked artistic skills. Pre-Engineering made me think, exposed me to different fields within engineering, is a high paying field, and allowed me to be hands on at the same time. After exploring all four majors, I chose Pre-Engineering. I participated in sports during my time in high school, running cross country as well as playing baseball and basketball. I was also able to earn A's and B's in my courses while balancing athletics.

There were three basketball teams at BCIT; Varsity,

Junior Varsity, and the Freshman squad. During my first year, I made the Freshman team, played as a starter, and midway through the season played a few Junior Varsity minutes. When the season was over, the entire starting five from the Freshman team was being trained for Junior Varsity and Varsity. We had off season practices and played in summer tournaments and different leagues with some of the returning Junior Varsity players. One summer league I'll never forget, was in Haddon Heights, NJ. Our team truly became a unit after playing together for so long and listening to the coaching that helped elevate our skills. We won just about every regular league game, breezing into the playoffs. There were two playoff rounds prior to the championship. We won the first playoff game, but the second round really challenged us. The whole game was close. Our opponent took the lead going into the fourth quarter. Our coach called a time out and gave us a talk that lit a fire in all of us. As the buzzer went off to start the final quarter, my coach yelled "defense wins games!" For us, that meant nobody crosses half court and that's exactly what happened during the first four minutes of the quarter. After several minutes of intense defense, we took the lead. As the final minutes of the game came, I got a steal and went straight to the basket for a layup. As I jumped to score, my leg was side swiped in the air, coming down to land flat on my left hip. When I hit the ground, all I heard was "ooooouuuu" from the crowd. To my surprise, I was ok. I finished out the game and we won. We only had one day to prepare for the championship game and my coaches wanted to use our time wisely, calling for a 2 hour practice the day before. When practice began, we started off doing full court defensive slides. No less than 2 minutes into the drill, I felt a pain I'd never felt before. My left hip and leg started to tighten up to the point where I could barely move it. I couldn't believe this was happening the day before the championship game. My coach made me sit out the rest of the practice and after a same day MRI and X-Ray, the doctor gave us news that I fractured my hip and strained my hip flexor. I was devastated. All the hard work I put in during the summer, all the time my coaches invested in me, all the time I spent growing my skills, it felt like it was all for nothing. I didn't understand why this had to happen now, just when my team became a strong unit and my game really started to excel. There was nothing I could do to change what had happened. The only remedy to heal a fractured hip and strained hip flexor is rest. No running, no lateral movements, no lifting weights, no basketball. When I broke the news to my coaches and teammates, they were just as shocked as I was. The next day, I was forced to sit the championship game out and was happy they won, even without me.

As an athlete, it was extremely frustrating to rest and resist the temptation of stepping on the court too soon. When the summer ended, I listened to the doctor and rested so I could be ready for tryouts my sophomore year.

The new school year started, and I was cleared for physical activity by my doctor. Cross country season always happened before basketball season and it felt good being able to run again, especially without any pain. I was even able to play basketball in gym class without any pain, but this was short lived. When basketball tryouts began, the hip pain returned. I was able to make it through tryouts but was hindered by this injury and didn't play as well as I had in the past. I made Junior Varsity, but my coaches and I knew I couldn't reach my full potential injured. At that time, basketball had consumed me, and I had to remember that there was much more to me than just sports. I was a Pre-Engineering major and loved to learn. If getting A's and B's came without thinking hard, I could only imagine how my grades would be if I pushed myself. The thought of excelling academically excited me. The possibilities of where I could go and what I could achieve seemed limitless. It was time for a mindset shift away from sports and into school.

4

TRANSITIONS

As the basketball season came to an end, my grades began to improve significantly. B's turned into A's and A's turned into A+'s. I took pride in all the work I did, and I refused to settle for anything less than an A. My mindset had completely changed about school as I began transitioning from a student-athlete, to a full-time student. At some point, we're all going to transition from one stage of life into the next, whether it be from childhood to adulthood, or from employees to business owners. According to Webster's dictionary, a transition is *"passage from one state, stage, subject, or place to another."* I can thank my hip injury for the transition I experienced.

At the end of my sophomore year, I had finished the semester with straight A's. At the forefront of my mind was being a good role model for my younger sister. It's not often that people show or tell you that it's cool to be smart, so I tried to lead by example. Going into my junior year, my love for basketball remained and I was able to make the team again. With my focus on academics, I was preparing for college by taking my SAT's and ACT's and looking at potential schools to attend. I took both exams twice until I got a score I was satisfied with. I even visited a college for the first time (Rutgers University) thanks to what some may call a second Mom, Ms. Myricks. At the beginning of my senior year, I met with my school's guidance counselor on a weekly basis to make sure I was doing everything I needed to, so I could be prepared for college. There's no such thing as a bad question, except questions that are not asked. I made sure I asked my counselor every question I could think of related college and my future. I found out that I qualified for the *New Jersey Stars Program*, which is a state program that allows NJ students with a cumulative GPA of 3.0 or higher and ranked in the top 15% of their class to attend two years of community college then transfer to a state university for another two years, tuition free. I couldn't believe how much my hard work was paying off.

I was accepted to all 10 universities I applied to. My top choice was Rutgers, The State University of New Jersey. One of the most credible and recognized schools in the world that would also save my family money with in-state tuition. I was excited to finally get away from home and experience life on my own but paying for college was a big concern for my Dad. I tried to ease his concern by laying out a plan of what I wanted to study, how long it would take me to graduate, and my expected career salary. I even leveraged how hard I've worked in high school over the years to get accepted to such a prestigious university. Coming from a working-class family, I knew my parents didn't have the money to pay for college, but I was willing to take out student loans and bet on myself. I knew I wouldn't fail and had the utmost belief in myself. While my mother was willing to support any decision I made, my father was not as convinced about Rutgers and wanted me to play it safe by going through the NJ Stars program, so I did.

Graduation approached and I was more excited for my friends going away for college then I was for myself. Although the NJ Stars program positioned me to receive free tuition, it came with a trade-off that deeply impacted my spirit and mental health. After spending my high school career carefully crafting my college plans, it truly hurt that I wouldn't be able to execute them. I couldn't help but wonder why I was being stopped from my dreams. All I needed was a cosigner for student loans but that was something was Dad wasn't willing to do.

As the school year came to an end, it was amazing to watch so many of my friends prepare for college. Some went to in-state universities, while others went out-of-state. It was a bittersweet feeling. With a graduating class of 279, my academic rank placed me at number 7, an accomplishment I'll never forget. A blessing in disguise was getting injured playing basketball, which helped spur my academic ambition and take my academics much more seriously. As someone who's always been active playing sports, it was hard to sit on the sideline. But as J. Cole said in his song "Love Yours" — there's beauty in struggle.

5

13TH GRADE

After high school, I started my collegiate career at a community college. If you've ever gone to community college, some people say it's better and helps acclimate you to the rigors of college, while others say it's like the "13th grade." I didn't know what to expect other than I would be taking general requirement courses that all NJ universities would accept as transfer credits. I didn't know who else from my graduating class would be attending the community college either. However, I did know that I wasn't going to be there for long and approached my first year with a plan that would allow all the credits I complete to be accepted by Rutgers.

My goal was to graduate from Rutgers with a degree in Exercise Science & Sports medicine. Having experience as a lifelong athlete and having to rehab from a previous serious injury inspired me to pursue this degree. Knowing that certain courses were transferable to Rutgers, I made an appointment with my guidance counselor before the semester started to ask questions about these courses. I wanted to know what classes I should take at the community college if I wanted to pursue Exercise Science & Sports Medicine. I also wanted to know what recommended schedule I should take to meet my timeline of transferring in two year.

Meeting with my counselor helped answer all my questions and provided a sense of relief. My counselor also pointed me to a very helpful website, Njtransfer.org, where I could check what courses are currently eligible for transfer credit in the New Jersey university system. This website quickly became my bible and it gave me insight into course selection and a recommended order to pair classes. By the time my first semester began, I had mapped out my entire course schedule for the next two years of my community college experience.

When the first day of classes started, I was shocked at how fast students came and left campus. When the day started, the parking lot and hallways were packed. When classes ended for the day, the campus became a ghost town, with the parking lot, hallways, and entire buildings completely empty. People came to class to learn and left class to go to work, including myself. I had to keep a job to pay for gas to get to and from school. Being at a community college, I was looking forward to seeing a community presence on campus, but I didn't. All I saw was the speed of people coming and leaving throughout the day. A lot of students looked at least 10 years older than I was and not a recent high school graduate. The only social interactions that took place were inside the classroom. I knew this wasn't the type of learning environment I wanted to be in. It wasn't quite the college experience I was hoping for.

As the weeks went on, my desire to go to campus dwindled and my motivation to go to Rutgers grew. I wanted to be around people my age and who have similar interests to me. I yearned to be in a more traditional collegiate setting. By the time my first semester came to an end, my Mom could tell I was miserable. She knew that I wanted bigger and better. One day during the winter break she came into my room and asked me "son, how's school going?" "It's ok" I replied. "Just ok? Are you learning the things you want to?" she asked. "I guess so. All the things in the major that I want to learn are at Rutgers though" I replied. Then she asked me something that she never asked me before, "are you happy son?" I replied, "what do you mean?" She replied "are you happy? I've been seeing you go to school, go to work, come home and just stay in your room. That's not like you. When me or your sister comes into your room, you're quick to rush us out. You've been isolating yourself." I was surprised at how much she noticed my behavior change, changes that I hadn't even noticed myself. I thought really long and hard about that question and finally replied, "no, I'm not happy. Community college isn't what I expected. I'm not really around people on campus, let along people my age, besides the classroom. Everyone pretty much just comes to school and leaves. I've been ready to go away to Rutgers." My Mom could see the truth in my face as I spoke. She felt the mental anguish I was going through. I'll never forget, in that moment she responded and told me "ok, we're going to work everything out so you can go to Rutgers. Don't worry about your Dad. Your happiness is all I'm concerned about. Even if I have to pay out of my own pocket, you're going to get into that school, and this stays between us for now, you hear me?" I couldn't believe my ears. "Yes Ma'am" I replied. It felt like God had answered my prayers because Lord knows staying at community college for another year would have driven me crazy. Sometimes all you need is one ally with you to go far, and I had the best ally anyone could've asked for, my Mom.

6

EXECUTE

As the second semester of my first year at community college quickly approached, I turned my attention to Rutgers and my future enrollment. My Mom and I used the original 4-year plan I created as the framework for planning enrollment, and then we focused on ironing out a few more things, especially the financial part. She agreed to be the cosigner for my student loans and we even found out how to set up a payment plan with the university. If it's one thing we know how to do, it's how to find out information. We found out everything we needed by simply calling the school and asking the right questions. Once we had everything in place, it was time to reapply to the school and execute our plan. According to Webster's dictionary, execute means *"to carry out fully or put completely into effect"*, and that's exactly what we did.

During my second semester in community college, I began to slowly enjoy everything. Not because I was looking forward to going to Rutgers next fall, but because I was actually around people my age in the classroom and everyone spoke and enjoyed each other's company. I couldn't help but wonder why it took 2 semesters to feel a sense of community on campus, but I didn't think too hard about it. Halfway through the semester, I got my acceptance letter from Rutgers. It was a surreal feeling, and much more intense than the first time I was accepted there.

Joyfully, I called my Mom and told her about getting accepted into school again. While she was happy for me, she also struck a serious tone when she reminded me not to say anything about it to my Dad until we received the financial aid offer. Roughly one month passed and we finally received the offer. It was more than we expected, but there still was a balance left to be paid. After setting up the payment plan to resolve the balance, I officially accepted my offer to attend Rutgers. I couldn't believe all the hard work I did paid off again, with a tremendous assist from my mother. With everything in place regarding enrollment and financial aid, my mother and I told Dad about our plan. As we began to detail everything, there was a tension in the room that became noticeable between the three of us. When we were done explaining everything, he responded in a dismissive and irritable manner, stating only "this was ya'll plan, so I'm expecting ya'll to handle everything, including paying for it." Hearing words like that motivated me even more to succeed. Sometimes when we accept the reality in front of us, it makes life easier to deal with, seeing what's true before your eyes. When you see what's true, it helps to eliminate false expectations, making it much harder for you to be affected while following your truth.

A few days went by and I could feel a silent tension developing towards my mom and I from my dad. I didn't think too much about it because I knew I had my mom in my corner. She told me to focus on finishing the school year strong so I could enter Rutgers with a high GPA. I finished the school year with all A's and 1 B and made the Dean's list. When the summer started, I was excited to start a new chapter of my life away from home, at my dream school. One thing that I was worried about was having everything I needed to go away. Packing for college, I realized I needed quite a few household items like toiletry, linens, cooking supplies, the list went on. I asked my Mom how and when we were going to get everything I needed, and she told me not to worry because we're going to have a Trunk Party. I had never heard of trunk parties before, but I was grateful that my family and friends were supporting me off to college by bringing things I would need as gifts.

We had the trunk party in July, 1 month before the start of the fall semester. It was bittersweet knowing that I would soon have to leave my family and friends, but it was exciting to see so much support for this next phase in my life. Everyone brought items that I would need for the upcoming school year. The afternoon before move-in day I did my last round of goodbyes to my close family and friends. Everyone was excited for me to start and experience this new journey in my life. In the morning of move-in day, I made sure I had everything and got ready to leave. In the car ride to the school, I couldn't help but smile in a state of bliss and think to myself "wow, the plan is in full effect."

7

NEW BEGINNINGS

As a first-generation college student and first in my family to attend a division 1 university, I fully embraced the adversity I went through and was ready to start strong during my first semester at Rutgers. Arriving on campus was a moment I'll never forget. I didn't have the traditional dorm life experience as I was accepted into a living learning community, where people who have similar academic interests live together. I moved into a suite with 3 rooms, a living room, and private bathroom — housing 6 people in total. My roommate and I were the only 2 Black people in that suite, and just 2 of 6 Black people in the entire community. Culture shock was a real thing that day but having at least 1 other person that looked like me was comforting.

During the first week of classes, I made a bunch of new friends and was introduced to other people almost instantly. I had a work study job at the gym and the campus was exactly what I imagined it to be; vibrant, energetic, innovative and cultured. The only thing that bothered me was where I lived. It lacked the positive things I felt in other areas on campus. I didn't feel the cultural vibration in the building I lived in. How can one function or perform at a high level when home is an uncomfortable one? Outside of sleeping and getting dressed, I didn't stay in my room much. I knew that living in the learning community wasn't for me. Sure, we had similar academic interests, but outside of that we had very little in common. It wasn't as comfortable as I thought. I knew where my people were, what campuses and dorms they were in, and that's where I wanted to be. I made up my mind that I wanted to move into the new apartment buildings on Livingston Campus and started doing research to see how I could switch my housing. By staying curious, I managed to find the contact information I needed. After a few email exchanges and a short phone call, I was placed on the waiting list to move into the new apartments and about a week later, I was able to move in.

When I moved into the apartment, it was the kind of space I needed — my own room, a shared kitchen, 2 bathrooms and 3 other roommates who looked just like me. I was happy to be there, and it was closer to my work study job at the gym. My job at the gym was one of a kind. My building manager, Dwayne, and I formed a great working relationship, filled with meaningful conversations. One talk always stood out. He came into the gym, a little happier than usual, and started talking to me about the job offers he had received. He must have had at least 5 job offers lined up. This was the first time I ever even engaged with someone that looks like me with multiple job offers, let along my building manager. The more I listened to him talk about how grateful he was for the opportunities, the sooner I realized that it was only the beginning of the fall semester. I asked him "how do you have all of these job offers, and the school year just started?" He replied to me and said "there's a misconception about college, that you have to go to school and then get a job. If you do it in that order, you have to wait to find a job after school when really you could land a job while you're already in school. When you're in college, you should want to go to school to be set up to graduate, rather than graduate and find a job. When you're set up to graduate, jobs are knocking at your door before you even finish your senior year, and you can set yourself up to graduate with professional experience under your belt. Things like internships, apprenticeships, and fellowships get you the industry experience you need to add to your resume and build meaningful relationships. You can't get that if you just attend classes and turn in your homework." That was a conversation that completely changed my outlook on college. I didn't want to go to school to graduate and find a job anymore, I wanted to be set up to graduate.

As the semester went on, I met more and more people and eventually found my tribe, friends who have been through thick and thin with me to this day. We meet different people through different stages in life. No one friend group is above another. They're all family to me and have all met my family. Friendship is essential to the soul. In an age where instant gratification is praised, it's important to remember all the new beginnings you've had, all the people who were there to support you, and all your friends and family. The length of a friendship doesn't determine the strength of it. If it weren't for my friends in college, I would've never known about all the resources available to students at Rutgers and how valuable these were in my college career.

As my undergrad years went on, I was progressing through my major faster than expected. Exercise Science & Sports Medicine was intensive but, with proper planning, along with summer school, I managed to put myself in position to graduate a semester early. The summer before my senior year, I managed to secure an internship with Princeton University as a Strength and Conditioning Coach. My dream was to be an Athletic Coach for a major league sports team. The internship was everything I expected it to be. I got to create workout plans informed by science, train college athletes, and learn new workouts myself. My staff manager was helpful throughout the internship. When the summer was coming to an end, my managers and I had a very candid conversation about the career's duties, responsibilities, day to day life, and salary outlook. They told me that I'd have to really love being a Strength and Conditioning Coach to be one when the internship started, but in this last conversation they explained to me why. The working hours range from 5am - 12pm — far from your average 9 to 5. To be eligible for consideration in a university setting, you not only have to have a master's degree, but you would have to have a good relationship with others at the college and network strategically. Additionally, the expected career salary only ranges from 30K - 50k. As much as I loved exercise science, everything I found out about the career outlook didn't align to my 4-year plan or expected salary. The only thing that made sense was understanding why someone would have to really love their job to be in this field.

At the end of my internship, I was somewhat disheartened. Sports was always something I loved and had my eyes set on working in, but the career outlook didn't align with my values or expectations. I had to rethink my plan and find a new major to study. I wasn't looking to study something too intensive like Nuclear Physics, although they make a lot of money. I was looking for alignment. Work that wouldn't feel like work. I had to dig deep and evaluate myself and things I liked. After a few hours of soul searching and looking through the degree catalog it finally clicked in my head. I thought back to when I was younger when my Mom introduced me to technology. I then recognized that I was already a natural when it came to understanding technology. The things that we are naturally gifted and talented in that others find difficult are our *Super Powers*. President Barack Obama is naturally a gifted speaker, making him one of the best public speakers in history. Madam C. J. Walker was naturally talented in hair care and business, making her the wealthiest Black woman of her time. Since I was naturally gifted in technology, making the choice to change my major was easy.

8

ALIGNMENT

Who would have thought that I'd switch my major right before my senior year of college? Probably nobody, myself included. But I'm a firm believer that everything happens for a reason, and I switched my major to align myself with my natural gifts. Life has a way of making us pursue things that look good but looks aren't the only thing that matters. Happiness, passion, and alignment outweigh how things look. According to Webster's dictionary, alignment is *"an arrangement of groups or forces in relation to one another."* I've always had a comfortable relationship with technology, it made perfect sense to realign with something I naturally understood.

After assessing the major requirements and mapping out how long it would take me to complete, I made the request to switch my major to Information Technology right before the term started. Although changing my major cost me an extra semester of school, the benefit more than outweighed the cost. I would have to take 18 credits for 3 semesters to finish by fall 2015 and was fine with that. As with any new major, I also had to go through the introductory courses for the program. Oddly, it felt refreshing to be a senior in courses with mostly younger peers. I was excited to go to class every day and I truly loved learning about technology. Knowing that I would need internship experience to differentiate myself from others, I headed straight to a career fair after only being in the major for less than one semester. The good thing about most college career fairs is that students can view employers that will be attending prior to the event, allowing you time to research certain companies that you might find attractive. I studied every company that would be at the career fair that was offering internships to seniors in my industry and made sure I knew facts about each company. I also went to career services to get feedback on my resume and how I could best present myself to potential employers. After preparing as best as I could, it was off to the career fair.

On the day of the career fair, I arrived in a suit and tie with plenty of copies of my resume and business cards ready to pass out. I felt prepared, confident, and ready to land an internship. Before entering the fair I made a list of the companies I wanted to talk to, ranging from companies I was very interested in to those I was less excited about. One by one, I approached each company introducing myself, sharing my story, and telling the recruiters why

I'm interested in their organization. One thing I knew for sure was that each recruiter would remember my story; after all, you'd have to be crazy or really passionate to switch your major your senior year. At the career fair there was one company in particular where I spoke with the recruiters longer than I did with any other company. The synergy between the company and my background was strong. It was a technology company in the healthcare industry, and I was an information technology major with a background in exercise science. After the recruiter and I finished talking, we exchanged contact information and I had a feeling that I would be working there. The universe will send you certain signals to confirm your heart's desires and the only thing you have to do is take action. Action allows us to take steps towards our goals, and a goal without action is nothing more than a dream. My goal was to have a job in place before graduating, just like my building manager taught me, and I took all the proper actions necessary.

After the career fair, I emailed all the recruiters I spoke to with a follow-up thank you email. If it's one thing I learned in undergrad, it's how important emails are, especially follow-up emails with others who can add value to your network. Each email sent was personally customized to each recruiter so that they could recognize how genuine I was. When you personalize emails others will be able to sense your authenticity. Most of the recruiters I reached out to responded to my emails, while some didn't. But there was really only one email I was waiting for, from the technology company in the healthcare industry. As eager as I was to send another follow-up email, I restrained myself from doing it thanks to advice from my career services advisor. My advisor had told me before the career fair that when someone sends multiple follow-up emails to thank a recruiter, they tend to be perceived as desperate and that wasn't how I wanted to be pictured at all.

About two weeks went by and I finally received a reply from the recruiter; I was being invited to an initial first round interview. You can only imagine how excited I was. On the day of the interview, I walked in with confidence, tenacity and ambition. My strategy was to turn the interview into a conversation by being personable and getting to know the person interviewing me. When I met my interviewer, we started by getting to know one another. I found out that he was not only an employee for the company, but also an adjunct professor at Rutgers. The interview went great and I must have left a good impression with him because I received an email for a second round of interviews. I scheduled my interview for the next week so I could have time to prepare. The day of the interview, I was escorted to a conference room, and before the interview started, I was told that someone else would be joining. Group interviews are something I've always known companies do, but this was the first time I've ever been in one. After the first interview was done, I was told that there would be two more people coming into the room to interview me to expedite the interviewing process. When the two men came into the room, there was immediate synergy in the air. It was only supposed to last for 30- minutes but ended up being closer to an hour. It didn't feel like an interview at all, it felt like a great conversation.

As the fall semester continued, I noticed that no other job I talked to at the career fair invited me to an interview. I couldn't help but wonder why and I began to ask my friends and family about it. They offered a lot of comforting words and insight from their experience. That was all I needed to calm my nerves. Before the semester ended, I got another email from the company I interviewed for and the subject line said "Congratulations." I opened the email and the first sentence told me that I was accepted in the next internship cohort for the summer of 2015. None of this would have been possible had I not personally reflected and aligned my-self to information technology. Sometimes, we have to take one step back to take three steps forward.

9

WINTER BREAK,
OR NOT

Every student loves winter break. It's a time to relax and enjoy a break from school. For me, the work didn't stop. After my first semester in my new major, I realized that the program was arranged to be an introduction to the different subcategories that fell under the information technology umbrella. As great as the program was, my gut told me a bachelor's degree alone wouldn't help me reach my goals. According to the National Center of Education Statistics, only 8.2% of Black people have advanced degrees such as a masters or doctoral degree, compared to Caucasians with 12.1%, and non-Hispanic White alone with 13.5%. It lit a fire in me and made me want to pursue another degree to inspire others and equip myself with more. I figured I'd be able to figure out what exactly I wanted to do in the field going through a master's program. After I set my mind to it, it was time to do the research!

Searching the school's website allowed me to find out what advanced degrees it offered in my field. I came across one that really grabbed my attention, the Master of Library and Information Science program. It is a prestigious program, ranked the #6 Library and Information Science program in the nation. Before the spring semester started, I made sure to prepare myself for this advanced degree. I emailed professors I had good relationships with, asking for letters of recommendation to enter the program. I turned to prepare for the GRE and looked up different resources like Khan Academy to get ready for the exam. They say you can never be right about predicting the future, but you can always be right about being prepared, and prepared I was.

When the spring semester started, I was on a mission to set myself up for success and make my family proud. I thought back and reflected on my entire undergrad journey. It felt like only yesterday I was moving my things on campus. My mind was on my graduating semester even though it was a ways away. Forward thinkers can have a tendency to be mentally in the future, and that's exactly where my mind was. A slight wave of anxiety related to graduating grew, but I think that is natural for any student, even those who are set up to graduate with job offers.

A few weeks into the semester and it was time to take the GRE. The test took about 5 hours to complete and I couldn't have been prouder of myself. I did pretty well on all parts of the exam and was pleased with the results. I honestly believe I wouldn't have done so well without the resources I used for preparation. Whoever said free resources don't deliver the same quality as paid ones did not tell the truth. The truth is, you can get the same amount of quality from free resources when you put the right amount of effort and time in. The only costs associated with free resources are time and effort, as with anything else in life. After I received my GRE scores it was time to turn in my graduate school application, which was a milestone. Not only am I a first-generation college student in my family, but I would be the first one to attend graduate school also. As the spring semester continued, the only goal I had to focus on now was making sure I kept my grades up in my last two semesters.

10

MANIFEST

When the spring semester came to an end, it was time to start the internship. The first day started bright and early at 8:30am and there were about 30 students in the cohort. We all met in a huge orientation room where we were offered breakfast and refreshments. Throughout the morning, we met with different leaders in the organization, such as managers, supervisors and the CEO. It was an honor and quite humbling to meet these leaders and take in valuable information. As the day went on, we received a pleasant surprise in being notified that we would be paid for the internship. I didn't expect to get paid for the internship because it wasn't stated in the initial welcome letter. Sometimes when you don't see what you expect and still say yes to opportunity, you receive more than what you were expecting.

When the first day of orientation ended, I couldn't wait to tell my friends and family. They weren't just happy for me; they were my support system as well. As time went on, I began to learn the corporate culture. Interns had access to the entire building, allowing us to connect with other employees. I've always heard that corporate spaces don't truly represent diversity but experiencing it firsthand for the first time was almost surreal. I was one of two Black people in the internship. I knew at that point I would need to work twice as hard for me and for other underrepresented people who would come after me. Day by day, week by week, I made sure I showed up on time and was one of the last to leave. I managed to build a great reputation for myself. My team and I were part of a summer project that our manager encouraged us to finish before leaving. As time went on, the team progressed, and we managed to finish it before the internship ended. We were even given the opportunity to present our work to other managers in the building. After our initial presentation, my manager praised me for being so well spoken and leveraged the team to learn from me. I gave all my gratitude to Rutgers for allowing me to develop my public speaking skills and learned that other students on my team had never done presentations while in college. As shocked as I was, I was thankful to have the educational experience I did. As the internship wound down, our manager asked us if we'd like to present our work to the CEO. We quickly said yes and blew the CEO away with our work.

On the final day of the internship, everyone in my cohort was talking about full-time offer letters. With this being my first internship and corporate experience, I didn't know that the company would extend offer letters at all. As curious as I was, I asked questions to other students in my cohort about the offer letters to see what information they knew. I found out that most companies extend offer letters to interns about two weeks after it ends if you performed well and that our company was well known for making offer letters to interns. I was excited and relieved knowing that I had nothing to worry about because I worked hard the entire summer. I thought back on the entire internship and how I made sure to overachieve. Had I not kept that mentality, I probably would have been a little worried finding out that the company only extends offer letters to people who performed well, but I didn't have a worry in sight.

On our last day of the internship, the cohort was called into the conference room where we first met our managers. The managers gave us a final talk, discussing how proud they were of us, what they learned working with us, and how important it is to continue our professional development as we move towards graduating college. When the talks ended, everyone turned in our company equipment and was gifted with a farewell gift bag. I said my goodbyes to all of my new colleagues and friends and left to head back to my house on campus. After a long summer of working hard, it felt good to have a few weeks to relax before my final semester of undergrad started.

As the summer wound down, I took the final week to

spend time with my family and friends. It's always good to show love to the ones that have been there supporting you. When you have the time, make sure to take care of your tribe and show them appreciation. It doesn't have to be anything lavish or extensive, it can be something as simple as spending quality time with them, and that's exactly what I did. On the last Friday before school started, I checked my email and saw two things I'd never forget. The first was from my internship, extending a full-time job offer to me after a summer of high-quality work. The second was an acceptance letter into graduate school at Rutgers for the Master of Library and Information Science program. Everything that I had put my mind and energy to came to fruition that day.

When my last fall season of undergrad started, I decided to enroll in an extra semester, becoming a member of Omega Psi Phi Fraternity Incorporated and graduating in the spring of 2016. I started working full time that summer and started graduate school as a part-time student when the fall came. After three years of juggling school and work, I graduated with my master's in Library and Information Science. I believed I could do it, I put the effort into it, and manifested it.

When we believe we can do things, ask the universe or your higher power for it, put action towards receiving it, and you'll receive it. The universe will not tell you no. No is not in its dictionary. The universe will only tell you yes, not right now, or it has something better for you. That's the power of manifestation. We can do anything we put our minds to. Once we have a goal in mind, action is the only requirement to receive it. A goal without action is only a dream, and the only time we dream is when we're asleep at night. Nobody knows how to carry out every action, which is why curiosity is essential. Curiosity can help you achieve any goal you have in mind. It's the action of seeking and following your heart's desire. However, curiosity alone is not enough. Emotional intelligence is the map that helps guide your curiosity from making any wrong turns. It's the GPS that helps you navigate hard conversations and difficult situations. Life is full of difficult and unexpected situations, but we can avoid most by forward thinking. Forward thinking allows us to think about things holistically and to create a plan for the future, a roadmap to follow, and a short or long-term goal to achieve. It allows us to see things from a bird's eye view. It gives us something to work towards, rather than just experiencing life as it is. Keeping your eyes on the prize is good, but using your peripheral vision is even better. Tunnel vision can blind us from the things that exist around and beyond ourselves, like friends and family. Being mindful and reciprocating love to the ones that support us is critical to maintaining healthy and good relationships with family and friends. Mindfulness also helps us recognize when adjustments and transitions are needed. Being able to adjust is important, so that we don't feel disrupted when our plans don't go the way we intended. It also helps us align things that were not aligned before, whether if it's a sport or a college major. When we have alignment in ourselves, from our beliefs, to our hearts, to our mind, to our actions, anything is possible. Lifelong curiosity can be your biggest ally when you use it properly. I hope the stories and lessons from my journey can help you along yours.

Always remember, stay curious.

AFTERWORD

Curiosity is a gift that everyone has. If nurtured properly, it can help you achieve any goal. I am a testament to what curiosity can offer when used in ways that promote self-help, which is why I've decided to share my story to encourage others to follow their curiosity. No matter where you are in life right now, you can still reach your dreams by answering these few questions and putting action behind them.

1) What are your life goals?

2) What are you passionate about?

3) What things in life intrigue you?

4) How can you learn more about the things you are interested in?

5) What trade skills or abilities do you have that are easy for you but may be hard for others to do?

6) How can you use those skills or abilities to help you reach your goals?

After you have answered these questions, I encourage you to use this as your guide along your journey in life.

REFERENCES

[1] Gino, F., Aramaki, C., & Todd B. Kashdan David J. Disabato Fallon R. Goodman Carl Naughton. (2018, December 18). Why Curiosity Matters. Retrieved August 25, 2020, from https://hbr.org/2018/09/curiosity

[2] Perry, B. D., Dr. (n.d.). Why Young Children Are Curious. Retrieved August 25, 2020, from https://www.scholastic.com/teachers/articles/teaching-content/why-young-children-are-curious/

[3] Merriam-Webster. (n.d.). Curiosity. In Merriam-Webster.com dictionary. Retrieved August 25, 2020, from https://www.merriam-webster.com/dictionary/curiosity

[4] "Intellectual Freedom and Censorship Q & A", American Library Association, May 29, 2007. http://www.ala.org/advocacy/intfreedom/censorship/faq (Accessed August 25, 2020)
Document ID: e8ae9ed7-a469-f0d4-adf0-f2770d2ca8e8

[5] Emotional Intelligence. (n.d.). Retrieved August 25, 2020, from https://www.psychologytoday.com/us/basics/emotional-intelligence

[6] Merriam-Webster. (n.d.). Forward-thinking. In Merriam-Webster.com dictionary. Retrieved August 25, 2020, from https://www.merriam-webster.com/dictionary/forward-thinking

[7] Merriam-Webster. (n.d.). Transition. In Merriam-Webster.com dictionary. Retrieved August 25, 2020, from https://www.merriam-webster.com/dictionary/transition

[8] Merriam-Webster. (n.d.). Execute. In Merriam-Webster.com dictionary. Retrieved August 25, 2020, from https://www.merriam-webster.com/dictionary/execute

[9] Merriam-Webster. (n.d.). Alignment. In Merriam-Webster.com dictionary. Retrieved August 25, 2020, from https://www.merriam-webster.com/dictionary/alignment

[10] Ryan, Camille L, and Kurt Bauman. "Educational Attainment in the United States: 2015." U.S. Census Bureau (2015)., www.census.gov/content/dam/Census/library/publications/2016/demo/p20-578.pdf.